THE
2010
GRIFFIN
POETRY
PRIZE
ANTHOLOGY

THE 2010 GRIFFIN POETRY PRIZE ANTHOLOGY

A SELECTION OF THE SHORTLIST

Edited by A. F. MORITZ

ANANSI

This edition published in 2010 by
House of Anansi Press Inc.
110 Spadina Avenue, Suite 801
Toronto, ON, M5V 2K4
Tel. 416-363-4343
Fax 416-363-1017
www.anansi.ca

Distributed in Canada by
HarperCollins Canada Ltd.
1995 Markham Road
Scarborough, ON, M1B 5M8
Toll free tel. 1-800-387-0117

Distributed in the United States by
Publishers Group West
1700 Fourth Street
Berkeley, CA 94710
Toll free tel. 1-800-788-3123

House of Anansi Press is committed to protecting our natural environment. As part of our efforts, this book is printed on paper that contains 100% post-consumer recycled fibres, is acid-free, and is processed chlorine-free.

14 13 12 11 10   1 2 3 4 5

Library and Archives Canada Cataloguing in Publication

Cataloguing data available from Library and Archives Canada

Library of Congress Control Number: 2010924080

Cover design: Gwenaël Rattke
Text design: Ingrid Paulson
Typesetting: Sari Naworynski

Canada Council   Conseil des Arts
for the Arts   du Canada

ONTARIO ARTS COUNCIL
CONSEIL DES ARTS DE L'ONTARIO

We acknowledge for their financial support of our publishing program the Canada Council for the Arts, the Ontario Arts Council, and the Government of Canada through the Canada Book Fund.

Printed and bound in Canada

CONTENTS

CANADIAN FINALISTS

PREFACE

It is a daunting honour to serve as a judge for the Griffin prize. Daunting because of the boxes that arrive; first one, then another and another and another — so many slim volumes! — and daunting because of the requirement to judge poetry at all. And in such variety — we received books from almost all the English-speaking world, and from original languages as diverse as Arabic, Spanish, Italian...How to do it? Where to begin?

You begin by opening a box (and with that first glimpse you appreciate the beauty of the books as objects, so full credit to those publishers who take such care). You open a box then suddenly you're sitting among piles of books, and then you open a book. Then another, then another...

So, what you do is read and listen — and what you hear are conversations and accusations and songs. You hear lyrics and exclamations, griefs and intimacies and truths; worked in all the shapes language can take.

At first it felt churlish to judge — every good book of poems is an act of valour, and intelligence, and as poets ourselves we all knew what it feels like to send a book out into the world. But we had to get on with it and in our separate places we three judges considered almost 400 books, in two categories, International and Canadian. We all fall into habits and preferences, so one of the stimulations of judging was being obliged to read beyond one's usual sphere, to discover poets one had never encountered before. Therefore, surrounded by opened boxes, tottering piles of books, we judges were in a privileged position: we were granted an overview of the poetry published in the English-speaking world in one year, the tenth of the new millennium, the tenth since Scott Griffin inaugurated his prize. We set about it with old-fashioned reading and feeling and thinking, and then, by the wonders of modern computing and telephony, we discussed it, and arrived at a shortlist of seven. To arrive at that list meant excluding very many books; but privately we all made discoveries, we each found poets new to us.

At length we chose the books we did because they delighted or intrigued or moved us. They were not only accomplished — there were many accomplished books to consider — but these ones sparkled. We chose these books because these poets had taken risks with the important things, with soul, memory, love, history, landscape — but had triumphed.

To write is a risk and so is to read. We are all fond of saying poetry is the Cinderella art. Overlooked, even mocked — but wherever there is human community there is poetry. We've had chant and song since the Paleolithic. We are the species with language, poetry is what we do. It won't go away. If it is sidelined in the short term by interests apparently more powerful, maybe it's because they are afraid of that risk: you open a book of poems, you risk your heart and soul.

It's to Scott Griffin's credit that he makes that mutual, risky approach, poet and reader, more possible than it would have been. The Griffin Poetry Prize, while honouring the poets, primarily says: look here. And as its judges for 2010 it's our honour to be able to say — take a chance on these books in particular, because we believe these will repay you handsomely.

We went in daunted but emerged, I think, with our humanity enhanced, refreshed with the possibilities of language. We felt what Seamus Heaney called "the redress of poetry" and were strengthened by it. Now we can hand over to the wider public, saying: if you try nothing else this year, try these. Take a chance. You might be moved and delighted too.

Kathleen Jamie, March 2010

EDITOR'S NOTE

Coming after the selection of seven superb books by the judges, the editing of this anthology was easy and difficult. Easy because there were power and beauty on every page, and (to echo Wordsworth) whatever I chose, I could scarcely have missed my way. Difficult because few were the poems that seemed possible to exclude: each one cried out when it was cut — or was that me? Another quandary: not only was Valérie Rouzeau's elegy translated by Susan Wicks a unified work, but there was no missing the cohesiveness of all these books. Each displayed its own dramatic balance between the individual poem and the whole book as focal unit of composition.

The choices here show the power and beauty mentioned, and ought to signal how much more waits in each original volume. I hope they also suggest the accumulative richness of each, and the striking coincidences among these generous poets. For all their differences, and for all their truthful troubling of the waters ("To love is to consent to distance," writes Solie), they make me think primarily the thought that Padraic Colum once had in contemplating the folk sources of the sometimes brutal fairy tales: "But they were at one in their love for certain things — for human good nature, for enterprise, wisdom and devotion, for the genius through which men are drawn to the far-off and the superior — the Golden Tree, the Water of Life, the Matchless Maiden."

John Glenday notes that "Etching of a Line of Trees" is based on the etching "Eye of the Wind" by Bill Duncan, and that "The Kelp Eaters" draws on G. W. Steller's *Journal of a Voyage with Bering 1741–1742*, tr. M. A. Engel and O. W. Frost (1998). Eiléan

Ní Chuilleanáin states that her "In the Desert" takes its image of snakes in a well from *Arabesques* (2006), tr. Ibrahim Mumayiz, a selection of classical Arabic poetry. Most pages in *Cold Spring in Winter* have the form of two short poems, one suspended from the top margin and one rising from the bottom as in the final selection here. Kate Hall writes, "The line 'manipulating the bodies they ride in' (in 'Little Essay on Genetics') and the title 'Survival Machine' are borrowed from Richard Dawkins." As editor of *The Best Canadian Poetry in English 2009* I have previously anthologized Page's "Coal and Roses — A Triple Glosa" and Solie's "Tractor" and so, signature poems though these two are, I've excluded them here in order to present others equally striking.

A. F. Moritz, April 2010

INTERNATIONAL
FINALISTS

JOHN GLENDAY

Grain

In John Glenday's work we hear a calm, confiding voice. This is a mature work, Glenday writes slowly and out of necessity, and in *Grain,* his third collection, he has achieved a work of wry spiritual authority which never preaches or instructs. Alert to Scottish landscapes and turns of phrase, these poems never send readers away bewildered or confused. We are drawn in to shared confidences. His highly crafted lyrics are like wrought iron, strong but delicate, with a care for assonance and cadence. He listens carefully to the language he works in. They're also playful: a tin can, a peculiar fish, invented translations, made-up saints all can suggest poems. It's refreshing to discover a poet whose work is earthly, full of rivers and hills and islands, but where old ideas like "love" and "soul" have not been banished. *Grain* is the work of an unhurried craftsman; John Glenday has made poems of understated integrity and humanity. "Sun through the sea / sea in the heart / heart in its noust / nothing is lost."

The River

This is my formula for the fall of things:
we come to a river we always knew we'd have to cross.
It ferries the twilight down through fieldworks

of corn and half-blown sunflowers.
The only sounds, one lost cicada calling to itself
and the piping of a bird that will never have a name.

Now tell me there is a pause
where we know there should be an end;
then tell me you too imagined it this way

with our shadows never quite touching the river
and the river never quite reaching the sea.

St Orage

Preserve us, St Orage, you whose image stares down
on our weed-snagged railway sidings and choked
factory yards; whose relics crumble in a cardboard box
in a hampered lock-up somewhere. We await your word.

St Eadfast and St Alwart, we rely on you
to indicate the Good Path, however stony.
Lead us not into that rock-strewn gully
clogged with St Randed's bones.

Oh Lord, we know your faithful
knew more deaths than we had fingers —
St Ifle and St Rangle and St Arving and St Ab, all
flew into your mercy through their disparate anguishes.

But most of all, remember us yourselves,
forgotten saints we here commemorate:
St Agger of the drunken brawling praise;
St Ainless, martyred on the lopped branch of his perfect life;

St Anza, stunned by her own reverberating song;
and blameless, maculate St Igmata, dead and forgiving child,
who even in the crib, they say, held up her little punctured hands
in wonder and in ignorance, and cried.

A Westray Prayer

i.m. Mike and Barbara Heasman

Let us now give thanks
for these salt-blown

wind-burned pastures
where oatgrass and timothy
shrink from the harrow of the sea

where Scotland at long last
wearies of muttering its own name
where we may begin

to believe we have always known
what someone in his wisdom
must have meant

when he gave us everything
and told us nothing.

Etching of a Line of Trees

i.m. John Goodfellow Glenday

I carved out the careful absence of a hill and a hill grew.
I cut away the fabric of the trees
and the trees stood shivering in the darkness.

When I had burned off the last syllables of wind,
a fresh wind rose and lingered.
But because I could not bring myself

to remove you from that hill,
you are no longer there. How wonderful it is
that neither of us managed to survive

when it was love that surely pulled the burr
and love that gnawed its own shape from the burnished air
and love that shaped that absent wind against a tree.

Some shadow's hands moved with my hands
and everything I touched was turned to darkness
and everything I could not touch was light.

Stranger

Today, I am a new man,
a stranger in the town that bore me.

How simple it is to become a ghost —
just one word, one gesture, and we slip

through the fretwork of other people's lives
as easily as water through a stone.

Just for today, if I were to pass myself in the street
I wouldn't even raise my hat, or say hello.

The Afterlife

Because I could I did—build her I mean—from bits I found, the scraps of being no one else would have—harvested organs, glands that set the balance, patchwork features still the shape of who they were before they weren't, all hooked to a sack of blood and made to go somewhat. Bones hinged in their proper order, muscles flinched, the milk set in her eyes (a close match, not a pair). Somehow it worked. A marvel. God knows how. You should have seen me gaff the weather at its worst, all broken lights and wattage, then earth the brilliance through her. Took this for a show of love though she kicked with a reek of burn. It straddled every sinew, grounded at last in her opening face. One lid went back, she gazed up through my downward gaze, through the scaffolding of lights and instruments, on into overarching mirk. Then just as the current died the grey rag of her lips tore open for a moment and the air, forced through her throat's reed, broke with a play of notes, almost like song.

The Kelp Eaters

Hydrodamalis gigas

These beasts are four fathoms long, but perfectly gentle.
They roam the shallower waters like sea-cattle

and graze on the waving flags of kelp.
At the slightest wound their innards will flop

out with a great hissing sound,
but they have not yet grown to fear mankind:

no matter how many of their number might be killed,
they never try to swim away, they are so mild.

When one is speared, its neighbours will rush in
and struggle to draw out the harpoon

with the blades of their little hooves.
They almost seem to have a grasp of what it is to love.

I once watched a bull return to its butchered
mate two days in a row, butting its flensed hide

and calling out quietly across the shingle till the darkness fell.
The flesh on the small calves tastes as sweet as veal

and their fat is pleasantly coloured,
like the best Dutch butter.

The females are furnished with long, black teats.
When brushed hard with a fingertip

even on the dead
they will grow firm and the sweet milk bleed.

from 'Journal of a Voyage with Bering 1741–1742'
by Georg Wilhelm Steller

The Ugly

I love you as I love the Hatchetfish,
the Allmouth, the Angler,
the Sawbelly and Wolf-eel,
the Stoplight Loosejaw, the Fangtooth;

all our sweet bathypelagic ones,
and especially those too terrible or sly
even for Latin names; who staple
their menfolk to the vagina's hide

like scorched purses, stiff with seed;
whom God built to trawl
endless cathedrals of darkness,
their bland eyes gaping like sores;

who would choke down hunger itself,
had it pith and gristle enough;
who carry on their foreheads
the trembling light of the world.

Ark

Did we really believe
our love could have survived
on that boat something or other
had us build of spavined cedar
pitched and thatched against the flood,
with two of nothing but ourselves on board —
no raven to hoist behind the rain,
no dove returning with a sprig of green?

Island Song

I cannot see my mother's face;
no longer know my father's name.
It's the forgetting of the world
keeps me sane.

A stranger's laugh, a neighbour's death;
my wife's despair, my daughter's grief.
It's the forgetting of the world
gives me breath.

The hungry, old, surrounding sea,
heaves at a field's worn edge in me.
It's the forgetting of the world
sets us free.

For Lucie

born 5 December 2005

How apt it was we named you
for the light: no more than a small light, mind

— a spunk; a spill; a stub of tallow
cradled against the draft

while our stooped shadows lengthen
and fall away behind.

Here's to you, then, and to us,
to your world and to ours.

We raise you towards the dark.
May you make of it something else.

LOUISE GLÜCK

A Village Life

In *A Village Life*, Louise Glück presents us with a choir of voices whose song enacts and contemplates our human quest for the very happiness that — as if instinctively — we refuse. The result is a restlessness that seems never to leave us, as Glück suggests in "In the Café": "It's natural to be tired of earth. / When you've been dead this long, you'll probably be tired of heaven. / You do what you can do in a place / but after a while you exhaust that place, / so you long for rescue." This clarity of wisdom everywhere punctuates these poems which, even as they concern restlessness, are cast in long lines shot through with imagery of pristine, archetypal simplicity producing a cinematic stillness; one thinks of the camera in a Bergman film. The tension between that stillness and the subject of restlessness produces a resonance that builds even as it shifts like thought, like the light and dark that constantly fall across the village itself. As for the village, it seems ultimately to be the human spirit itself, replete with hopes realized and dashed, dreams without resolution, memories to which we return, often enough, to our regret, and too late. *A Village Life* is a tour-de-force of imagination and artistry, and shows Glück putting her considerable powers to new challenges.

First Snow

Like a child, the earth's going to sleep,
or so the story goes.

But I'm not tired, it says.
And the mother says, You may not be tired but I'm tired —

You can see it in her face, everyone can.
So the snow has to fall, sleep has to come.
Because the mother's sick to death of her life
and needs silence.

Fatigue

All winter he sleeps.
Then he gets up, he shaves —
it takes a long time to become a man again,
his face in the mirror bristles with dark hair.

The earth now is like a woman, waiting for him.
A great hopefulness — that's what binds them together,
himself and this woman.

Now he has to work all day to prove he deserves what he has.
Midday: he's tired, he's thirsty.
But if he quits now he'll have nothing.

The sweat covering his back and arms
is like his life pouring out of him
with nothing replacing it.

He works like an animal, then
like a machine, with no feeling.
But the bond will never break
though the earth fights back now, wild in the summer heat —

He squats down, letting the dirt run through his fingers.

The sun goes down, the dark comes.
Now that summer's over, the earth is hard, cold;
by the road, a few isolated fires burn.

Nothing remains of love,
only estrangement and hatred.

A Night in Spring

They told her she came out of a hole in her mother
but really it's impossible to believe
something so delicate could come out of something
so fat — her mother naked
looks like a pig. She wants to think
the children telling her were making fun of her ignorance;
they think they can tell her anything
because she doesn't come from the country, where people know
    these things.

She wants the subject to be finished, dead. It troubles her
to picture this space in her mother's body,
releasing human beings now and again,
first hiding them, then dropping them into the world,

and all along drugging them, inspiring the same feelings
she attaches to her bed, this sense of solitude, this calm,
this sense of being unique —

Maybe her mother still has these feelings.
This could explain why she never sees
the great differences between the two of them

because at one point they *were* the same person —

She sees her face in the mirror, the small nose
sunk in fat, and at the same time she hears
the children's laughter as they tell her
it doesn't start in the face, stupid,
it starts in the body —

At night in bed, she pulls the quilt as high as possible,
up to her neck —

She has found this thing, a self,
and come to cherish it,
and now it will be packed away in flesh and lost —

And she feels her mother did this to her, meant this to happen.
Because whatever she may try to do with her mind,
her body will disobey,
that its complacency, its finality, will make her mind invisible,
no one will see —

Very gently, she moves the sheet aside.
And under it, there is her body, still beautiful and new
with no marks anywhere. And it seems to her still
identical to her mind, so consistent with it as to seem
transparent, almost,

and once again
she falls in love with it and vows to protect it.

Solitude

It's very dark today; through the rain,
the mountain isn't visible. The only sound
is rain, driving life underground.
And with the rain, cold comes.
There will be no moon tonight, no stars.

The wind rose at night;
all morning it lashed against the wheat —
at noon it ended. But the storm went on,
soaking the dry fields, then flooding them —

The earth has vanished.
There's nothing to see, only the rain
gleaming against the dark windows.
This is the resting place, where nothing moves —

Now we return to what we were,
animals living in darkness
without language or vision —

Nothing proves I'm alive.
There is only the rain, the rain is endless.

Abundance

A cool wind blows on summer evenings, stirring the wheat.
The wheat bends, the leaves of the peach trees
rustle in the night ahead.

In the dark, a boy's crossing the field:
for the first time, he's touched a girl
so he walks home a man, with a man's hungers.

Slowly the fruit ripens —
baskets and baskets from a single tree
so some rots every year
and for a few weeks there's too much:
before and after, nothing.

Between the rows of wheat
you can see the mice, flashing and scurrying
across the earth, though the wheat towers above them,
churning as the summer wind blows.

The moon is full. A strange sound
comes from the field — maybe the wind.

But for the mice it's a night like any summer night.
Fruit and grain: a time of abundance.
Nobody dies, nobody goes hungry.

No sound except the roar of the wheat.

Threshing

The sky's light behind the mountain
though the sun is gone — this light
is like the sun's shadow, passing over the earth.

Before, when the sun was high,
you couldn't look at the sky or you'd go blind.
That time of day, the men don't work.
They lie in the shade, waiting, resting;
their undershirts are stained with sweat.

But under the trees it's cool,
like the flask of water that gets passed around.
A green awning's over their heads, blocking the sun.
No talk, just the leaves rustling in the heat,
the sound of the water moving from hand to hand.

This hour or two is the best time of day.
Not asleep, not awake, not drunk,
and the women far away
so that the day becomes suddenly calm, quiet and expansive,
without the women's turbulence.

The men lie under their canopy, apart from the heat,
as though the work were done.
Beyond the fields, the river's soundless, motionless —
scum mottles the surface.

To a man, they know when the hour's gone.
The flask gets put away, the bread, if there's bread.
The leaves darken a little, the shadows change.
The sun's moving again, taking the men along,
regardless of their preferences.

Above the fields, the heat's fierce still, even in decline.
The machines stand where they were left,
patient, waiting for the men's return.

The sky's bright, but twilight is coming.
The wheat has to be threshed; many hours remain
before the work is finished.
And afterward, walking home through the fields,
dealing with the evening.

So much time best forgotten.
Tense, unable to sleep, the woman's soft body
always shifting closer —
That time in the woods: that was reality.
This is the dream.

A Village Life

The death and uncertainty that await me
as they await all men, the shadows evaluating me
because it can take time to destroy a human being,
the element of suspense
needs to be preserved —

On Sundays I walk my neighbor's dog
so she can go to church to pray for her sick mother.

The dog waits for me in the doorway. Summer and winter
we walk the same road, early morning, at the base of the escarpment.
Sometimes the dog gets away from me — for a moment or two,
I can't see him behind some trees. He's very proud of this,
this trick he brings out occasionally, and gives up again
as a favor to me —

Afterward, I go back to my house to gather firewood.

I keep in my mind images from each walk:
monarda growing by the roadside;
in early spring, the dog chasing the little gray mice,

so for a while it seems possible
not to think of the hold of the body weakening, the ratio
of the body to the void shifting,

and the prayers becoming prayers for the dead.

Midday, the church bells finished. Light in excess:
still, fog blankets the meadow, so you can't see
the mountain in the distance, covered with snow and ice.

When it appears again, my neighbor thinks
her prayers are answered. So much light she can't control her
    happiness —
it has to burst out in language. *Hello*, she yells, as though
that is her best translation.

She believes in the Virgin the way I believe in the mountain,
though in one case the fog never lifts.
But each person stores his hope in a different place.

I make my soup, I pour my glass of wine.
I'm tense, like a child approaching adolescence.
Soon it will be decided for certain what you are,
one thing, a boy or girl. Not both any longer.
And the child thinks: I want to have a say in what happens.
But the child has no say whatsoever.

When I was a child, I did not foresee this.

Later, the sun sets, the shadows gather,
rustling the low bushes like animals just awake for the night.
Inside, there's only firelight. It fades slowly;
now only the heaviest wood's still
flickering across the shelves of instruments.
I hear music coming from them sometimes,
even locked in their cases.

When I was a bird, I believed I would be a man.
That's the flute. And the horn answers,
when I was a man, I cried out to be a bird.
Then the music vanishes. And the secret it confides in me
vanishes also.

In the window, the moon is hanging over the earth,
meaningless but full of messages.

It's dead, it's always been dead,
but it pretends to be something else,
burning like a star, and convincingly, so that you feel sometimes
it could actually make something grow on earth.

If there's an image of the soul, I think that's what it is.

I move through the dark as though it were natural to me,
as though I were already a factor in it.
Tranquil and still, the day dawns.
On market day, I go to the market with my lettuces.

EILÉAN NÍ CHUILLEANÁIN

The Sun-fish

This beguiling poet opens many doors onto multiple worlds. From the outset, with the startling imagery of "The Witch in the Wardrobe" — a "fluent pantry," where "the silk scarves came flying at her face like a car wash" — we are in a shifting realm, both real and otherworldly. The effect of her impressionistic style is like watching a photograph as it develops. *The Sun-fish* contains approaches to family and political history, thwarted pilgrimages in which Ní Chuilleanáin poses many questions — not always directly — and often chooses to leave the questions themselves unresolved, allowing them to resonate meaningfully past the actual poem's end. She is a truly imaginative poet, whose imagination is authoritative and transformative. She leads us into altered or emptied landscapes, such as that in "The Polio Epidemic," when children were kept indoors, but the poet escapes on a bicycle: "I sliced through miles of air / free as a plague angel descending / On places buses went . . ." Each poem is a world complete, and often they move between worlds, as in the beautiful "A Bridge Between Two Counties." These are potent poems, with dense, captivating sound and a certain magic that proves not only to be believable but necessary, in fact, to our understanding of the world around us.

Where the Pale Flower Flashes and Disappears

Then the waters folded over him
Their long leaves their ripple embrace
Dissolving the lines of his face
The sky crowded on top of him
The trees held the firmament up in its place
Their peacock spread
The last thing meeting his gaze.

The trees began their song the notes
Bound to the spot,
A repetitious air turning again
But strong enough
That the stunned mourners found
They were afoot they had walked outside
In the air although
Just now they felt themselves sinking
Into a grave.

Out of that dark they came and saw the trees —
Branches tense like dancers
Over their glass — they saw the roots,
A piercing grasp
That roved down, under and between the buried stones.

A Bridge Between Two Counties

The long bridge
Stretched between two counties
So they could never agree
How it should be kept

Standing at all
(In the mist in the darkness
Neither bank could be seen
When the three-day rain

The flood waters
Were rising below).
On that day I looked
Where the couple walked

A woman a small child
The child well wrapped
Becoming less visible
As they dodged left

Then right, weaving
Between the barrels and the planks
Placed there to slow the traffic
And something came

A brown human shape
And the woman paused and passed
The child's hand
To a glove and a sleeve

And very slowly
At first they moved away, were gone,
There was the mist,
The woman stood and seemed

To declare something
To the tide rocking below
And for the second time
In all my life I saw

The dry perfect leaf
Of memory stamped in its veins
The promise I heard
Val Kennedy making

At my sister's funeral
In his eightieth year: *She will live
Forever in my memory.* So her words
Floated out on the water consonants

Hardly visible in the mist vowels
Melting and the scatter of foam
Like the pebble damage
On a sheet of strong glass.

I watched the woman,
Memory holding the bridge in its place,
Until the child could reach the far side
And the adjoining county.

Come Back

Although there is no paper yet, no ink
There is already the hand
That moves, needing to write
Words never shouted from balconies of rock
Into the concave hills
To one far away, whose hair
On a collarbone resembles
That break in the dunes, that tufted ridge
He must have passed, faring away.

If the railway does not exist yet, there is, even
Now, a nostril to recognize
The smells of fatigue and arrival,
An ear cocked for the slow beginning,
Deliberated, of movement, wheels rolling.

If the telephone has not been invented
By anyone, still the woman in the scratchy shirt,
Strapped to her bed, on a dark evening,
With rain beginning outside, is sending
Impulses that sound and stop and ask
Again and again for help, from the one
Who is far away, slowly
Beginning her day's work,
Or, perhaps, from one already in his grave.

Michael and the Angel

Stop, said the angel. *Stop* doing what you were doing
    and listen.
Yes, you can taste the stew and add the salt
(Have you tried it with a touch of cinnamon?)
But listen to me while you're doing it.
I am not the one who found you
The work in the Telephone Exchange.
That was a different angel.
I am the angel who says *Remember*,
Do you remember, the taste of the wood-sorrel leaves
In the ditches on your way to the school? Go on,
Remember, how you found them
Piercing a lattice of green blades,
And their bitter juice. The grassy roads
That swung in and out of the shade
Passing a well or a graveyard,
The gaps and stiles on the chapel path —
Their windings, their changes of pace
Always escaping the casual watch you kept —
You must go back and look at them again,
And look again the next day, for they change,
There is new growth, or the dew is packed like a blanket.
Later come rose hips and the bloom of sloes,
And you must be there to see them. Your children will find
The sweet drop in the fuchsia flower, swallow it down;
They will run from the summer shower, but your work is
    to stay,
To hold the pose of the starved pikeman, grasping upright
The borrowed long ladder. After the rain
Dries off your shrinking shirt, the blue flower
Will shine up from the aftergrass where it nestled.
You will have to guess the size of the steam rising,

How it frees itself, sliding up off the field
At the time when the beeches are dropping their mast,
When the sloes are ripe in the hedge, you might still
Find the taste there, among the last of the grain.

Ballinascarthy

Is marach an dream úd Caithness dob' ag Gaeil a bhí an lá.
— Pádraig Óg Ó Scolaidhe

There, where the bard Ó Scolaidhe tells the loss
Of the great fight when the Croppies met the Caithness
Legion: the date, 1798, cut in brass,

The man driving the forklift truck said: Keep on
Straight up the road and you'll see the monument
And turn to your right. But when I had gone

Up the long hill to the cross of Kilnagros,
I saw only the spruces that had grown
Darkening green on either side of the stone.

After a mile I turned back and drove west, blinded
By dancing flaws in the light, as I passed
Under the planted trees, like dashed foam

Or the dashes of yellow and white on an old headstone.
Yet in that darkening light I saw the place,
Turned left and followed the falling road

For the graveyard. I searched for my great
Grandfather's name, Charles Cullinane, but I found
Only one Daniel, 1843, one headstone,

And in Kilmalooda I found Timothy's name
On a headstone in the long grass almost lost,
And Jeremiah's, and I found the name *Bence-Jones*,

1971, cut by Séamus Murphy who made my father's stone
In 1970, in the Botanics, and below that another name
In a different hand, Ken Thompson's, I recognized:

Ken Thompson carves the figure 9
In a different style, as in the stone he made
For my mother and her second husband in their Offaly grave.

I left the Bence-Joneses in the long grass
And drove back to the cross
And downhill again past the secret monument

To the dead of the great battle of Kilnagros
Where the spruces whistle to each other and the carved stone
   is lost.

In the Mountains

1

You are almost at the end of your journey;
Nobody has asked you for help
Since the child playing by the yellow gable
Who had lost her ball in the gully.
The broad linked chain still weighs down your pocket.

It is early in the mountains,
The mist thronged like blossom,
The grassy road to the harbour
Grey with dew, the branches
Loaded like a bride with embroidery.

2

Do you remember the dark night
When the voice cried from the yard
Asking for water, and you rose from the bed.
You were gone so long, I said to myself at last
As long as I live I will never ask who was there.

But now I want to ask that question.
I see you at the boundary stone and I need
To say the word that will bring her out of the trees:
Notice her: she limps to the field's edge —
A step, a clutch at the baldric, a hand to her hair.

The little stony stream divides forest from field.
She looks away. The wooded scene accentuates
The grace that says *Look — don't look* wavering
Like the spring breeze tossing the leaves, her draperies
Hesitant, her flexed foot on dappled gravel.

In the Desert

Almost day, looking down
From my high tower in the desert:
The sandstorm blows up,
Cuts my tower in half:
A crooked scarf of sand
As high as the window
That looks towards the mountains.
I cover my eyes
With my red scarf that slants
Wrapping my body
And when it is over
I look towards the desert
And I see him again
In the daybreak light
Still walking nearer —
He must be half blinded.

In the desert walking
I see them by the shining,
Reflection of dawn light,
Something bright sewn in the cloth
Worn on the head
Masking the face.
I see them glinting.

He is sand brown,
His clothes brown like sand.
Now he is closer
I see his shadow
As the dawn rises,
A bending shadow

And he nears the well
In the shade of the palm trees.

Coming to the well he lifts
Its wooden covering. Night
And coolness are still down there.
The snakes lie in the well, males
And females coiled together, wet.
Before he lowers his cup to drink
He salutes them saying, happy
Snakes, like the poor people,
Who have only the comfort men
And women find in each other.
Let me fill my cup, let me rest
Here in the shadow.

I hear him praying, I see him drink.
He lies down in the shadow.

To Niall Woods and Xenya Ostrovskaia,
married in Dublin on 9 September 2009

When you look out across the fields
And you both see the same star
Pitching its tent on the point of the steeple —
That is the time to set out on your journey,
With half a loaf and your mother's blessing.

Leave behind the places that you knew:
All that you leave behind you will find once more,
You will find it in the stories;
The sleeping beauty in her high tower
With her talking cat asleep
Solid beside her feet—you will see her again.

When the cat wakes up he will speak in Irish and Russian
And every night he will tell you a different tale
About the firebird that stole the golden apples,
Gone every morning out of the emperor's garden,
And about the King of Ireland's Son and the Enchanter's
    Daughter.

The story the cat does not know is the Book of Ruth
And I have no time to tell you how she fared
When she went out at night and she was afraid,
In the beginning of the barley harvest,
Or how she trusted to strangers and stood by her word:

You will have to trust me, she lived happily ever after.

SUSAN WICKS *(translator)*

VALÉRIE ROUZEAU

Cold Spring in Winter

Cold Spring in Winter is a sequence of poems occasioned by the death of the author's father. Valérie Rouzeau takes as her subject grief and the daily management of grief with its flowers, its armchairs, its special black clothes, its stupid idioms of consolation, its bundles of old *Scrap Merchant* magazines tied up with string (her father was a scrap metal dealer). The pages look like sentences of prose but they are often unpunctuated and the grammar invents itself in surprise jolts and slangy plunges. She makes the surface of the language dissolve and reform constantly as if it were aghast at itself. She pushes holes in the syntax and dives in and out of them, pulling the meaning after her. The tone seems controlled but it is the control of a shocked child. Overall a strange domestic dislocated voice and a crackling decisiveness of method. Grief is a very old room but here we walk into new air. The translation by Susan Wicks is alert, inventive, and gives a real sense of the level of linguistic risk and emotional force in Rouzeau's original.

You dying on the phone my mum he will not last the night see dad.

The train a dark rush under rain not last not die my father please oh please give me the get there soon.

Not deadying oh not desperish father everlast get up run fast —

Hand watch the time we've got to Vierzon outside it's tipping hail.

We miss each other I have no idea passing through Vierzon that in these train arrival times you've died.

Not die oh please but everlast until the nurses' corridor of white.

Until your bed as fast the engine into Lyon la Part-Dieu.

Until your forehead over now and all together in the little room and not forget.

My dad his lorry driving over the earth,
the sun warming his metals sorted neatly
into piles: copper and aluminium, zinc and
tin.

From high up there the magpies keep on
greeting.

The crane with caterpillar tracks is
making ruts where rainwater will like the
way it looks.

The grass is full of green insects singing
all over it in tune.

And it dances.

Stuck there in the ground not flinching
or thinking or anything.
And in the certain, final way of trees and
made of oak.
Like nothing nobody your life.
Snot-nosed in the goodbye hankies of my
dreams, suddenly put out.
Wind, nails.

We won't go mushrooming again the fog has swallowed everything the white goats and our baskets.

We won't be going to the enormous cities either which are highly organised grey whales our hearts would soon get lost.

Nor to the cinema or circus, the *café-concerts*, the cycle races.

We won't go we'll not be going any more no more than we won't go than we won't laugh we won't be laughing any more than we won't break up laughing.

Old old papers that César too has crushed, directories and corrugated cardboard, books and newsprint all together . . .

Or printers' blocks of crushed paper, ordinary bags (prices vary)?

Nickel from Severonickel, free-fall stainless steel in April.

Forget-me-not fittings from the Ugines Isbergues plant blue flower absolutely not: an avalanche of stainless leaf-thin sheets, that's all.

Complicated as a meeting of the 'grinders'' group of the national iron-workers' union.

A boat out of recycled drink-cans to cross the Pacific in.

Household ashes, broken glass.

More aluminium (pure, from saucepans), goose-feathers, white, half-white, lead whole empty batteries.

Red brass, bronze (from grapeshot, turning) other worn-out metals.

Pages from *The Scrap Merchant* that my father would read with care and tie in bundles as they dated.

And that makes two it's easy dad and me it's easy.

I count on him to make my peace with me.

Clouds go over us, toads croaking in the distance singing much more sweetly than they are.

My dad doesn't say a word the two of us are here but I'm the only one to have the wind blow through my hair and he's the only one not opening his eyes.

And I show him with my finger where the really puffed up song comes from of toads but he's familiar with the fable.

Clouds go over us our time, especially for me because I count them so.

My dad doesn't say a word we're different my dad and me and both of us left stranded.

Cold the cement poured cold into three equal slabs.

Three like pale nurses saying, 'Don't you know? Mr Rouzeau is . . . ?'

We'd crossed the rainy croaking fields of grass to quickly come and greet you 'passed away . . .' you that is Dédé with your friendly name of fatherly daddy Dédé.

Three syllables in chaos nurses all in chorus stunned that Dédé's dead and him so kind so ill.

'But he didn't feel himself go off he was asleep — rocked by the rain he went to sleep — he past away.'

You on your walk your hand in Mum's and goats in the distance beautiful, you feeling bad.

You on your native soil in little tiny steps that look quite weird.

You your little voice which drowns the goats' as walking baaack you feeling baaad saying secret tiny words of tenderness to Mum great tenderness and beautiful like her.

My father my father my father on earth as he is in summer wind in winter wind.

Oh my father in earth as he is in never I parrot it back my father my father.

In winter in summer wind all over the earth in the wind of singing.

Child in the great green pines it was you who were whistling blowing child in the great white pines.

My father I tell you again in passing I'm chucking this flower high enough.

My two feet in your light-coloured gravel.

My hands for the flower or the bird.

It's the same old crock of a bird its drilling voice its broken wings.

Shoot in the air and ancient greeting to the windscreen where the star is none too pleased.

Ill-mooned horses wheeling empty as I go by.

Jump a black puddle made of oil both feet together.

Choice bits higgledy-piggledy cam-shafts, connecting rods.

Industrial metal-crushers quarantined on the workbench hammers, chisels.

Neatness of my father's things, the dawn starts up again through the window where the pathetic bird gets bored and lets me go.

I bring flowers.

They hold on to all the colours they have lovely young girl names.

They'll stay stuck in the ground there waiting for whole days.

Now I'm going.

You had lovely eyes my father but I've other places other things to see.

You've got my flowers I've got your smile we're quits.

Eyes all dirty fingers stiff with cold this morning I've.

Was grumpy with the postwoman on her bike in my nightdress took me by surprise her ring.

Clean now dusted down in the sun admiring the tulips on their way out and the peony's beautiful buds.

And the beautiful budding peony starting again and I won't write any more to my father underneath the earth like an onion.

CANADIAN
FINALISTS

KATE HALL

The Certainty Dream

There should be an award for a person who, from within the confines of this grand funny country, can treat the topics of life, dreams, death, winter, and animals without earnestness. Kate Hall's book is called *The Certainty Dream* and it has what appear to be three homemade helicopters on the cover. The helicopters are in fact oil cans lashed to egg beaters and are held together by the good hopes of two tiny humans waving at them from the lower margin of the cover. It is a summary image of Kate Hall's method and mood. What holds a poem together, what holds a dream together, is the mind of some person working within it to make sense, using the available means. Her means include lots of philosophers' names and sparkly bits of their thought, but these are not decoratively invoked, they are woven into the sense that she makes and the mood in which she makes it. I like the feeling her poems give that as we read them we are amidst an actual process of thought. And that this process takes place, as she says, in "the gigantic margin reserved for wrong guesses."

Dream in Which I Am Separated from Myself

I don't want to see the city through
myself anymore. I imagine an open body
stuck with pins and flags ready
for labelling. The city is a city of constant
sidewalk repairs and household renovations.
If I could lay my hands on the interior walls
I would know enough to miss myself.
The city is a city of streets named
after saints and explorers. On the dock
I am cold. I imagine myself
at an art gallery looking at installations
and not pretending there can be
any sort of understanding.
But somewhere the water
may meet the unseen shore
and someone like you believes
it happens. There
is a line where they touch.
I would like to speak
to that line and have it speak
to me in return.

Overnight a Horse Appeared

I crawled out of a war machine.
You didn't recognize it as such, but
I did. I held it and nurtured it
and fed it strange wooden apples from my purse.

To spend a lifetime waiting inside
a stick horse is to live with the confusion
between hollow and hallow. I've lived
in this one room my whole life.

It looks a lot like outside. A tiny farrier
by the red barn in the distance. Four horses waiting
to gather us up. We cannot see beyond them.
We coloured their coats

to explain the end to ourselves.
The red horse and the pale horse
and the other and there is hunger. A tiny farrier
on the horizon line. Meaning, it's time

to crawl back inside myself. As the wind,
I'm drawing these patterns in the sand.
Accept the horse as a dangerous gift
you find meaningful, the offering

before the first burning arrow is fired
into the city. It could have been
fireworks or lightning. For my horse and me,
it hardly matters. Though it will matter for you:

how you decide to read me or
whether you do. Overnight, one horse
will gather us. The equine sternum
a drawbridge to a corporeal castle

we are plotting inside. Four horses
released on the unsuspecting city. I am the only one left
inside the warhorse I am holding in my hands.
I will have to live with him, maybe

for him. I am ready
to practice non-participation.
I want this to be the last thing I'll ever do,
to stop here and say I'll go no further.

Poem to Renounce My Renouncing

My apologies for not titling you
Your Grace or *Captain* or
Father. In the end
you didn't call the unearthly
coast guard to pull me
from the shoal when I'd had enough
and couldn't drive the boat
home. Unfortunate as you will deem it,
I'm taking it all back, each little thing,
and placing it inside
the old blue steamer trunk. The one
with the faded orange tag, specifying
my name, destination, occupation:
tourist and instructs HOLD.
When my possessions are all there, together
as in the beginning, before
I learned to flush shit away and leave
myself empty and porcelain,
I'm going to climb inside
with all my crappy belongings and
breathe until I can't breathe
anymore. But permit me to hold on
to my wickedness. Just that.

The Lost-and-Found Box

We are waiting for the claimants to come. You would like to keep the purple umbrella. I would like to keep the orange tree. We're both hoping no one will claim the blue beat-up dictionary. The dead won't give anything away. They carefully pick through the big pile of junky objects while we crouch reverently in front of it. A crowd is fighting over the morning star and the evening star, but there's only one star in the box. It's stretched thin between them. Fault lines are emerging. People approach from every possible angle. Secretly, we're hoping for disaster — a chaotic free-for-all so we can make off with as much as our arms can hold. At the door, George Herbert describes an orange tree to the admission clerk. As Herbert glances around, I step in front of it and wave my arms like branches. I feel a little bad because he wants it for God, and I just want it for myself.

Quick Tour of the Cathedral

In dark churches, certain boxes
are locked. I'm one of those tourists,
when held back from the incorruptible
by an iron railing, jostles
for a peek at the small window
you can't really see through.
There's no one at the prayer candles.
We've lit all our wishes on fire
and they give off too much light.

On a commercial break I start wishing
the blue volleyball team will win.
When they do, the final point
is scored like this: the ball is a white streak
right down the line and no one
moves to receive it.

If they play again, it will not be today.
Today I have a lot to answer for.
Fifteen people are jumping but fifteen other people are crying
and only a fine webbing separates them.

I hope that something in the locked box
will make up for this. Is it a real heart?
A real heart would stink
and rot and fall apart. Behind us, fire
is sucking up wishes. It's melting
the pillars they're standing on.

Little Essay on Genetics

It's possible to love your mother
even though you're genetically deficient
and she's genetically deficient
and our deficiencies make a big hole
in the ground. Eventually each of us will have to decide
whether to get cremated or buried in a fancy casket.
Evolution is about the genes
manipulating the bodies they ride in.
Little girls wish for ponies
without realizing their parents
have already turned them into genetic horses.
We are encoded but we have not yet
completely broken ourselves.
Genes can turn on suddenly
like a light bulb. This is a cause of
cancer. God we are amazing
biological gadgets. They cross-bred
two strains of mice. The genes
are an instruction manual, an identity
machine. The rats are right; I am frighteningly
like my mother. We are hardly here.

Survival Machine

The container for water
and information. We drew on
rocks. We figured out the word
sea. We figured out the words
basin and *submarine*. I shattered
a glass washing the dishes. I banged it
against another and underwater
one of them had to give.
I used to be a great birdwatcher
until the kingfishers flew
away, and I missed them
and still understood nothing about flight
after examining the wing structure.
It's a beautifully invented design.
It's a consequence.
Extinction. Sea basin.
The kingfishers. Submarine.
In a dream disposable straws are used
to download and upload information —
a process involving invisible marine organisms,
soggy computer chips
and resurrected kingfishers which remain a mystery to me.
Evolution. You took off your black sweater
and went to bed naked.
It has never changed.
Right from the beginning
it has been what it is.
For water. The container.

The Shipping Container

There must be a method of transport
because there are regulations about the movement
of dangerous goods. You made me
a photocopy. I've started worrying about getting
the proper transportation certificate
which requires the inspector's signature,
which in turn requires believing there is
an inspector with the authority to okay me.
There are moments when a dog will hear
what you cannot. The bark is a warning
at ninety-two decibels. Because you hear nothing
moving out there, fear is vague and constant.
Quiet is a command that registers only seven decibels when
spoken aloud. I read your note about the beauty
of the immune system and the mathematics of the brain.
How would you like me to interpret
this love letter? It weighs next to nothing
and ends abruptly. It's true, the container
has great aesthetic value but I was really hoping
for a free watch with a rechargeable battery or
at least a better kind of nothingness.

Insomnia

If I were to sleep, it would be on an iron bed,
bolted to the floor in a bomb-proof concrete room
with twelve locks on the door.
I wouldn't ask for a mattress
or decorate. I wouldn't ask for beautiful.
I'd let the philosophers in,
but not into my bed.
They'd arrive cradling their brass instruments.
I might let them play
but only very softly and only if
they didn't fight or sing.

If I were to sleep, there wouldn't be any windows.
There would be a skylight,
but in the middle of the floor.
I'd press my face against the glass
and stare down at other floors upon floors upon floors . . .
I'd do a sleep dance right on top of the skylight.
It would be a new game.
It would involve amazing feats of sleep contortion.
It would involve letters.

If I were to sleep, I would be spread-eagled across the bed,
and even with the iron struts and screws cutting into my back,
I would protect the metal frame.
I would protect the springs.

P. K. PAGE

Coal and Roses

Though we were not to know it, *Coal and Roses* was the last book to be published by P. K. Page, appearing months before her death at the age of ninety-three. Therefore it marks the close of a long and creative life. How heartening to be reminded that creativity, zest, and curiosity can endure, even flourish, into great old age. *Coal and Roses* is wholly unusual and possibly unique. It's a collection of 21 *glosas,* a *glosa* being an intricate, difficult form. Each poem begins with four lines from another poet — Anna Akhmatova, Thom Gunn, Zbigniew Herbert, and Ted Hughes all feature — and those four lines are then spun and meditated upon by Page herself, to form a new poem, where every stanza closes with a line from the master. The result is a history of poetry, a kind of memoir, and an *homage* from one nearing life's end, to her forebears and colleagues. It is a fully achieved project, which does what literature does best — abolishes the borders of life and death, time and culture and language, and sets all in a great conversation.

The Age of Gold

And the first age was Gold.
Without laws, without law's enforcers.
This age understood and obeyed
What had created it.
  — "Creation," Ted Hughes

What was, before the world
no one can imagine
and then the Creator created
winds and skies and seas.
Earth, with its fruits and trees,
before the world was old,
blossomed in sweet profusion.
Fish and flesh and fowl
were, magically, manifold.
And the first age was Gold.

And man appeared, and woman
innocent, full of wonder.
Eden, one myth called it,
Paradise, another.
Whatever the name, it was
flawless, an age of glory,
golden, sun-filled, honeyed,
lacking both crime and cunning.
It was a consummate order —
without laws, without law's enforcers.

Day followed night, the sky
cloudless, the air sweet-scented.
Night followed day, the stars
bright — Orion striding,
Cygnus, the Southern Cross,
the Lesser Water Snake.
All in their proper places
linked to the earth and shining —
a cosmological guide
this age understood and obeyed.

Minerals, plants and all
animals and humans
behaved according to
their original design.
Birds in their flight and flowers,
trees multifoliate,
salt in the mine, and water —
each honoured and celebrated
harmonized with and trusted
what had created it.

Ah, by the Golden Lilies

... ah by the golden lilies,
the tepid, golden water,
the yellow butterflies
over the yellow roses ...
    — "Yellow Spring" (translator unknown), Juan Ramón Jiménez

Jiménez, but for the roses
you paint a Rio garden
where every golden morning
the golden sunlight spills
on my Brazilian breakfast —
coffee like bitter aloes
strawberry-fleshed papayas
the sensuous persimmon ...
My young head full of follies
ah, by the golden lilies.

Beneath the cassia boughs
where fallen yellow blossoms
reflect a mirror image
I barefoot in the petals
trample a yellow world
while small canaries flutter
over the lotus pond.
I trail my golden fingers —
for I am Midas' daughter —
in the tepid, golden water.

My blue and gold macaw
laughs his demented laughter
dilates his golden pupils —
a golden spider spins
a spangled golden web
for beauty-loving flies.
Above the cassia branches —
the cassia-coloured sun.
Above the yellow lilies —
the yellow butterflies.

Jiménez, I am freed
by all this golden clangour.
Jiménez, your roses
denote a falling sound
a sound that will not rhyme
with *sambas jocosos*
macumba, feijoada
Bahían *vatapá.*
A different sun disposes
over the yellow roses.

The Blue Guitar

They said, 'You have a blue guitar,
You do not play things as they are.'
The man replied, 'Things as they are
are changed upon the blue guitar.'
 — "The Blue Guitar," Wallace Stevens

I do my best to tell it true
a thing exceeding hard to do
or tell it slant as Emily
advises in her poetry,
and, colour blind, how can I know
if green is blue or cinnabar.
Find me a colour chart that I
can check against a summer sky.
My eye is on a distant star.
They said, 'You have a blue guitar.'

'I have,' the man replied, 'it's true.
The instrument I strum is blue
I strum my joy, I strum my pain
I strum the sun, I strum the rain.
But tell me, what is that to you?
You see things as you think they are.
Remove the mote within your ear
then talk to me of what you hear.'
They said, 'Go smoke a blue cigar!
You do not play things as they are.'

'Things as they are? Above? Below?
In hell or heaven? Fast or slow ... ?'
They silenced him. 'It's not about
philosophy, so cut it out.
We want the truth and not what you
are playing on the blue guitar.
So start again and play it straight
don't improvise, prevaricate.
Just play things as they really are.'
The man replied, 'Things as they are

are not the same as things that were
or will be in another year.
The literal is rarely true
for truth is old and truth is new
and faceted — a metaphor
for something higher than we are.
I play the truth of Everyman
I play the truth as best I can.
The things I play are better far
when changed upon the blue guitar.'

The Last Time

There is a line of Verlaine I shall not recall again,
There is a nearby street forbidden to my step,
There is a mirror that has seen me for the last time,
There is a door I have shut until the end of the world.
      — "Limits" (Anthony Kerrigan, tr.), Jorge Luis Borges

I have been an omnivorous reader, cereal boxes
when I was a child at breakfast, comic strips
and all those stories in the *Girls' Own Annual*
that arrived at Christmas year after year and then
historical novels, Henty and Hugh Walpole
(and let me not forget 'The Little Red Hen'!)
Soon I shall not remember in any detail —
the Arabian Nights, the Russians or D.H.L.
(When shall I totally not remember? When?)
There is a line of Verlaine I shall not recall again.

Everything slips away. The street I lived on
at the first address I ever learned by heart.
And all those years in barracks, teenage travels
England, Spain, and Fatima's Hand on doors.
The mysterious foreign world unfolded for me.
And places closer to home. Now their time is up.
Do they miss my footfall? My eager foolish heart?
Not only the streets of New York, the streets of London
and not only the path that leads uphill to the top,
there is a nearby street forbidden to my step.

And then there are mirrors in which I am forgotten.
Until puberty I was like a cat or dog
unable to see myself, but vanity came
with adolescence — 'does that ear stick out?'
And later, 'Am I beautiful enough to please him?'
And later still, 'My anti-wrinkle cream
is a total disaster.' I am grey, without lustre.
I refuse to look at myself in any glass.
Though I tell myself old age is not a crime,
there is a mirror that has seen me for the last time.

When will the end of the world, its trumpets blaring,
uplift the holy and take them home to heaven?
And what of us, the wicked, who were not taken?
Don't ask. There are a multitude of answers
all of them known to hospitals and prisons.
Shall I lie with my nails painted, my hair curled
awaiting my beloved, as of old?
Will darkness snuff me out in the blink of an eye?
or shall I, like Jorge Luis Borges, see only gold?
There is a door I have shut until the end of the world.

Green, How Much I Want You Green

Green, how much I want you green.
Great stars of white frost
come with the fish of darkness
that opens the road of dawn.
— "Somnambular Ballad" (Stephen Spender and G. L. Gili, trs.),
Federico Garcia Lorca

Landscape of crystals
rock salt and icebergs
white trees, white grasses,
hills forged from pale metals
padlock and freeze me
in the Pleistocene.
See my skin wither
heart become brittle
cast as the Snow Queen.
Green, how much I want you green.

Green oak, green ilex
green weeping willow
green grass and green clover
all my lost youth.
Come before springtime
before the brown locust
come like the rain
that blows in the night
and melts to fine dust
great stars of white frost.

Water, sweet water
chortling, running
the chinooks of my childhood
warm wind, the ripple
of icicles dripping
from my frozen palace.
How sweet the water
moonstones and vodka
poured from a chalice
with the fish of darkness.

Come water, come springtime
come my green lover
with a whistle of grass
to call me to clover.
A key for my lock
small flowers for my crown.
The Ice Age is over,
green moss and green lichen
will paint a green lawn
that opens the road of dawn.

KAREN SOLIE

Pigeon

"If virtue is love ordered and controlled, / its wild enemy has made a home in me. And if / desire injures the spirit, I am afflicted," says Karen Solie in one of *Pigeon*'s finest poems, "An Acolyte Reads *The Cloud of Unknowing.*" It's this particular affliction of desire — and the corrosive effects of human desire both upon ourselves and the world we inhabit — that Solie most often meditates upon in poems as humorous, often, as they are sobering. "Gone are the bad old good old days. Before us, / vast unfenced acres of decline," she says in "Prayers for the Sick." Solie forces us to look squarely at that decline, the landscapes we've ruined, the vistas we've cluttered, in service to a longing that, as she puts it, "hovers like billboards / over the expressway." The vision here is powerful, philosophical, intelligent, especially adept at pulling great wisdom from the ordinary — as when a tractor is found to manifest "fate, forged / like a pearl around the grit of centuries." It may be, as Solie suggests, that "the honourable life / is like timing. One might not have the talent for it." Among the greatest of Solie's talents, evident throughout the poems of *Pigeon*, is an ability to see at once into and through our daily struggle, often thwarted by our very selves, toward something like an honourable life.

The Girls

They stayed at home. They didn't go far.
Trends do not move them.
From picture windows of family homes

they cast wide gazes of manifest pragmatism:
hopeful and competent, boundlessly integrated,
fearless, enviable, eternal.

Vegas, Florida, Mexico, Florida, Vegas.
With children they travel backroads
in first and last light to ball fields

and arenas of the Dominion.
We have no children. We don't own,
but rent successively, relentlessly,

to no real end. The high-school reunion
was a disaster. Our husbands got wasted
and fought one another, then with an equanimity

we secretly despised, made up over
anthem rock, rye and water.
Our grudges are prehistoric and literal.

It seems they will survive us. The girls
share a table, each pitying the others their looks,
their men, their clothes, their lives.

The World of Plants

In the world of plants, there is no Airbus 380.
Yet they're reborn to us selflessly
in fossil fuels! People, we're at the centre
of a great mystery. Last night saw us
dragging through the clubs, their soggy
double-digit martinis and vocals that reek
of auto-tune, suspecting someone else's fun
was having us. We snuck back through
the hole in the wall that's the door
to the part of the house that we rent
and re-entered the good life —
innocence of the new-mown grass blades,
our neighbour who clears his piece of sidewalk
with a hose, endlessly,
while the available portfolio
of non-prescription medication expands softly
as the evening around us. Circling,
a red-tailed hawk pinpoints the moving detail
of his meal in the big picture. We love him
from afar. Soon, we will have to have him.

Our longing hovers like billboards
over the expressway, the same questions,
same answers, throughout each long night.
The lake accumulates what is given it,
until gradually, though it may not appear so,
its constitution is changed. One thing dies,
another takes its place, and an unknown
potential enters the world. Anyone
who spots the alien invader Asian
longhorned beetle in the neighbourhoods
is asked to report this immediately
to the city. Without our efforts, no tree is safe.
It's as if everybody always wants us to do something.
I'd like to see someone make us. Please,
someone, come on over here and make us.

Cave Bear

The longer dead, the more expensive.
Extinction adds value.
Value appreciates.
This may demonstrate a complex cultural mechanism
but in any case, buyers get interested.
And nothing's worth anything without the buyers.
No one knows that better
than the United Mine Workers of America.

A hired team catalogued the skeleton,
took it from its cave to put on the open market.
Retail bought it, flew it over to reassemble
and sell again. Imagine him
foraging low Croatian mountains in the Pleistocene
and now he's flying. Now propped at an aggressive posture
in the foyer of a tourist shop in the Canadian Rockies
and going for roughly forty.

The pit extends its undivided attention.
When the gas ignited off the slant at Hillcrest
Old Level One, 93 years ago
June, they were carried out by the hundreds,
alive or dead, the bratticemen, carpenters,
timbermen, rope-riders, hoistmen,
labourers, miners, all but me, Sidney Bainbridge,
the one man never found.

Casa Mendoza

On public transit, I rode to meet him in the lounge
    of an old motel on a busy through-road
            in east Etobicoke, south of the Nabisco factory
        and water treatment plant amid sports bars,
tarp shops, dealerships, and self-
        storage, one of a strip doomed by the geologic
                headway of condominiums aspiring to Miami
or Neo-Deco via Vegas. CCTV and gated
courtyards, lakeside. I was committed
        to change. Lingered in the parking lot and thought it oddly
                gracious, appropriate, private, with its rear

        views of The Beach and Silver Moon, both earmarked
for demolition, disused antennas upholstered
        in birds and the big oaks throwing their overcoats
                over everything: weeds
        flowering in vacant lots, heaved sidewalk
from which I'd just seen a pair of Scooby-Doo
        underpants, men's, size XXL, in the gutter. Nearby,
                the Hillcrest and North American, in hourly
        throes of cost-to-profit ratios, were going down
in a blaze of filmic neon. The dark little lobby
        was Spanish-themed, with something German

about it, and anachronistically panelled. I was out
of my depth. Running hot and cold. From the patio
overlooking the water, the city core
                appeared as background and setting
                        for what we were mixed up in. Even then,
        a Demonstration Centre had cropped up on the long
lawn, pink to orange in the failing light like a patient,
                worsening, a woman inside manning
                        the phones. Above that, little brown bats,
                though they flew in dwindling numbers, flew nonetheless.
We knew it couldn't last, and then it did.

The Ex-Lovers

They are ongoing, in mid-season. They have mathematical
implications. A frenzy of unsustainable practice
hung a residue in the atmosphere, as though
the affairs had burned coal in their heyday,
then went abruptly bankrupt. It got quiet.
Eons passed. They re-emerged with the gravity
of unearthed figures from the Bronze Age. Now,
honestly, they've never looked better.

We're all beginning to feel mildly historic, walking
arm in arm with our former selves through streets
that look noirish and literary, as desirable properties
gain on the not-so-desirable, and a civil
population minds its peace. Sometimes a moment
acutely revisited leaves us unable
to breathe. They could do that. How unkind
it all seems to us now, and how marvellous.

Geranium

It seemed needlessly cruel
that I couldn't coax even the hardiest,
homeliest, dullest of plants to grow
in the one west-facing window
of that place, with its air conditioner, sealed
with duct tape, that didn't work,
and its mouse-hole, stuffed with steel
wool, that did. And an equally
needless kindness even more
unbearable, that unexpected flowering
inside the cheap circumference
of the pot while I was nearly
bedridden, of seeds borne on a broad wind
that flew in, and volunteered.

An Acolyte Reads *The Cloud of Unknowing*

Aspiring, not to emptiness, but to continually empty
one's self as a stream pours into a larger body
what it receives from the watershed — how midway
it carves a bed in this life, a clarity of purpose —
never ends. Simone Weil starves herself to death
again and again in London while the great mystery
appears to me as through a pinhole camera: reduced,
inverted, harmless. It's hard to concentrate, living
between Fire Station 426 and the Catholic hospital,
though the man shouting on the steps of the drop-in centre
appears, as much as anyone could, to be heroically
wrestling himself free from reality, his pain the soul's
pain in knowing it exists. I have dissolved
like an aspirin in water watching a bee walk into
the foyer of a trumpet flower, in the momentary
solace of what has nothing to do with me, brief
harmony of particulars in their separate orbits,
before returning to my name, to memory's warehouse
and fleet of specialized vehicles, the heart's
repetitive stress fractures, faulty logic, its stupid
porchlight. If virtue is love ordered and controlled,
its wild enemy has made a home in me. And if
desire injures the spirit, I am afflicted. Rehearsing
philosophy's different temperaments — sanguine, contrary,
nervous, alien — one finds a great deal to fear.
A lake-effect snowstorm bypasses the ski hills,
knocks the power out of some innocent milltown.
The world chooses for us what we can't, or won't.

X

In the evening I go out
among the peoples of the earth,
buy a few things, and so forth.
Apartment blocks in their concrete
shoes follow me all the way
home. Nights, an infinite variety
of human experience across
forty-two channels. How can I

explain my intentions when I don't
even know how a radio works?
In the fact of your absence,
you are in some way here,
like a Beethoven sonata
or the value of x, the variable
when the outcome is unknown,
as always the outcome is unknown.

ABOUT THE POETS

JOHN GLENDAY was born in Monifieth, Scotland, in 1952. He attended the University of Edinburgh, where he studied literature and language for three years before transferring to a psychiatric nursing program. He worked as a psychiatric nurse in Dundee, Scotland, for twelve years. He is the author of two previous books of poetry. His first, *The Apple Ghost*, won a Scottish Arts Council Book Award; his second, *Undark*, was a Poetry Book Society Recommendation. His poems have been anthologized in the *Faber Book of Twentieth Century Scottish Poetry*, *The Firebox*, and *New British Poetry*. He lives in Cawdor, Scotland, where he works as an addictions counsellor.

LOUISE GLÜCK is the author of eleven books of poetry, including *The Wild Iris*, which won the Pulitzer Prize, and *The Triumph of Achilles*, which won the National Book Critics Circle Award, the *Boston Globe* Literary Press Award, and the Poetry Society of America's Melville Kane Award. Her other honours include the Bollingen Prize in Poetry, the Lannan Literary Award for Poetry, and fellowships from the Guggenheim and Rockefeller foundations and from the National Endowment for the Arts. She is a member of the American Academy and Institute of Arts and Letters, and in 1999 she was elected as Chancellor of the Academy of American Poets. She teaches at Yale University and lives in Cambridge, Massachusetts.

KATE HALL's poems have appeared in several journals, including *The Colorado Review, jubilant, Swerve, The Denver Quarterly, Open City, Verse, LIT,* and the *Boston Review.* She has won the Irving Layton Award and the David McKeen Award. She was co-editor of the Delirium Press chapbooks and co-hosted the Departure Reading Series in Montreal. In addition to the Griffin Poetry Prize, her debut collection *The Certainty Dream* is also a finalist for the Gerald Lampert Memorial Award. She teaches at McGill University and lives in Montreal.

EILÉAN NÍ CHUILLEANÁIN was born in Cork City, Ireland, in 1942. She is the author of ten books of poetry, and she has translated poets from Irish, Italian, and Romanian. Her numerous awards include the Patrick Kavanagh Award, the *Irish Times* Award for Poetry, and the O'Shaughnessy Award of the Irish-American Cultural Institute. She was a founding member of the literary journal *Cyphers*, Ireland's longest established literary periodical. She is a Fellow and Professor of English at Trinity College, Dublin, and a member of Aosdána. She is married to Macdara Woods and they have a son, Niall.

P. K. PAGE, one of Canada's most celebrated poets, was born in England and raised on the Canadian prairies. She was the author of numerous books, including volumes of poetry, a novel, selected short stories, books for children, and a memoir entitled *Brazilian Journal.* A two-volume edition of Page's collected poems, *The Hidden Room,* was published in 1997, and her acclaimed collection *Planet Earth: Poems Selected and New* was published in 2002 and was a finalist for the 2003 Griffin Poetry Prize. She has won the Governor General's Literary Award for Poetry and been appointed a Companion of the Order of Canada. In 2006 she was made a Fellow of the Royal Society of Canada, and she held honorary degrees from the University of Victoria, University of Calgary, University of Guelph, Simon Fraser University, and University of Toronto. P. K. Page died on January 14, 2010.

VALÉRIE ROUZEAU was born in Burgundy, France, in 1967. She has published a dozen collections of poems and translated volumes from Sylvia Plath, William Carlos Williams, Ted Hughes, and the photographer Duane Michals. She is the editor of a review of poetry for children called *dans la lune,* and she frequently holds public readings, poetry workshops in schools, and radio broadcasts. She lives in Saint-Ouen, a small town outside of Paris.

KAREN SOLIE's first collection of poems, *Short Haul Engine,* won the Dorothy Livesay Poetry Prize and was a finalist for the 2002 Griffin Poetry Prize, the ReLit Award, and the Gerald Lampert Memorial Award. Her second collection, *Modern and Normal,* was a finalist for the Trillium Book Award for Poetry. In addition to being a finalist for the 2010 Griffin Poetry Prize, her third collection, *Pigeon,* is also a finalist for the Pat Lowther Memorial Award and was named a *Globe and Mail* Top 100 Book. She is a native of Saskatchewan and now lives in Toronto.

SUSAN WICKS is a poet and novelist. She was born in Kent, England, in 1947. She is the author of five collections of poetry, including *The Clever Daughter,* which was a finalist for the T. S. Eliot and Forward Poetry Prizes, and *Singing Underwater,* which won the Aldeburgh Poetry Festival Prize. She has lived and worked in France, Ireland, and the United States and taught at the University of Dijon, University College Dublin, and University of Kent. Her most recent book of poems, *De-iced,* was published in 2007, and a book of short stories, *Roll Up for the Arabian Derby,* was published in 2008.

ACKNOWLEDGEMENTS

The publisher thanks the following for their kind permission to reprint the work contained in this volume:

The selections from *Grain* by John Glenday are reprinted by permission of Picador.

The selections from *A Village Life* by Louise Glück are reprinted by permission of Farrar, Straus, and Giroux.

The selections from *The Certainty Dream* by Kate Hall are reprinted by permission of Coach House Books.

The selections from *The Sun-fish* by Eiléan Ní Chuilleanáin are reprinted by permission of The Gallery Press.

The selections from *Coal and Roses* by P. K. Page are reprinted by permission of The Porcupine's Quill.

The selections from *Cold Spring in Winter* by Valérie Rouzeau, translated by Susan Wicks, are reprinted by permission of Arc Publications.

The selections from *Pigeon* by Karen Solie are reprinted by permission of House of Anansi Press Inc.